CONTENTS

INTRODUCTION

Did you know that stories of mermaids have been around for more than 3,000 years? These beautiful, mythical creatures are hugely popular today, and this craft book is a must-have for all wannabe mermaids (and mermen too, of course). The book includes 15 projects to kit you out from head to tail, including dress-up crafts like the Mermaid Tail, Triton's Crown, and Shell Necklace; toys like the Aquarium Puppets and Meryl the Mermaid; decorative projects such as the Clamshell Trinket Box, Reef Wreath, and Mermaid Blanket; and ideas for an Under-the-sea Party with a showstopper cake that's really easy to make.

The projects are designed to be made by children and adults together. All the projects have simple step-by-step instructions with accompanying photos, so you need never get stuck. You will find all the templates you need at the back of the book.

Bear in mind that the materials, colors, and embellishments in this book are just suggestions. You can follow the instructions to the letter if you like, but we'd encourage you to improvise by using things you already have to hand and letting the children steer the project. They will love the end result much more if they have picked the colors and have done the cutting, painting, and sticking themselves.

Our kids all wanted mermaid birthday parties this year, so we've had a lot of practice seeing what mermaid-themed crafts worked with our kids and their friends. We hope we have produced crafts that your children will love as much as ours did. They were very happy we were making this book and helped us out with all the projects. In fact, we had to make several shimmery pencil cases and a tail for each of them!

Happy mermaid crafting, and visit our blog, www.littlebuttondiaries.com, for more inspiration!

TOOLS AND MATERIALS

Most of the projects in this book use items that can be found around the home or that are easily purchased online and in craft stores. It's best to use what you have and improvise for a personal touch. The tools and materials below are useful for the projects in this book and for crafting with kids in general.

Fabric

Shimmery and sequined fabrics are perfect for creating a scaly effect. We particularly love reversible sequined fabric, which you can pick up cheaply from online retailers. Felt and fleece are fantastic materials for children's crafts as they don't fray so you can sew projects without having to hide the raw edges first.

Paints

Acrylic paint is ideal for adding strong, permanent color to your projects. Cover all clothing and surfaces when painting with acrylics as they will stain clothes. You can use children's paints if you like but bear in mind that the end result probably won't last as long.

Sewing machine

Several projects in this book are created using a sewing machine, and we would recommend one for quick and sturdy results. Although very young children can't use a machine by themselves, they can sit on your lap and help to guide the fabric through, and they love to press the buttons.

Air-drying clay

This is great for kids to get their hands on, as it's easy to mold and work with. It can be painted and varnished once dry.

Craft foam

This is a fantastic material for children to craft with as it is more durable than card and you can easily draw on it and cut it with scissors.

Shells, gems, beads, and sequins

A lot of the projects in the book have had sparkle added with shells, gems, and beads. You can easily buy these supplies online or from craft stores.

Yarn and trimmings

Yarn is a great material for adding hair to projects and for making pompoms with, while a selection of ribbons and trimmings is always handy for adding finishing touches to projects.

Craft rummage box

Keep a box full of interesting things that you might otherwise recycle or throw out. Kids get a lot of pleasure from diving into the box, seeing what they can pull out, and turning it into something super. A shoebox, cardboard tubes, egg cartons, and fabric scraps have all been transformed in this book with the help of a little paint and a glue stick (and maybe a parent in the background with a glue gun!).

FISHTAIL PENCIL CASE

Reversible sequined fabric – with sequins that can be smoothed one way and then the other for a color-change effect – is the perfect fabric for wannabe mermaids. You will need a sewing machine with a zipper foot for this project and access to an oven for the shrink plastic zipper pull.

You will need

- Scissors
- Two-way sequin fabric, 8 x 12in (20 x 30cm)
- Blue cotton fabric for lining, 8 x 12in (20 x 30cm)
- Gold faux leather, 6 x 8in (15 x 20cm)
- Masking tape
- Pencil
- Sewing thread in contrasting color
- 8in (20cm) zipper
- Sewing machine with zipper foot
- Pins
- Needle
- Shrink plastic, 8 x 12in (20 x 30cm)
- Permanent pens or coloring pencils
- Hole punch
- Craft varnish
- Split ring

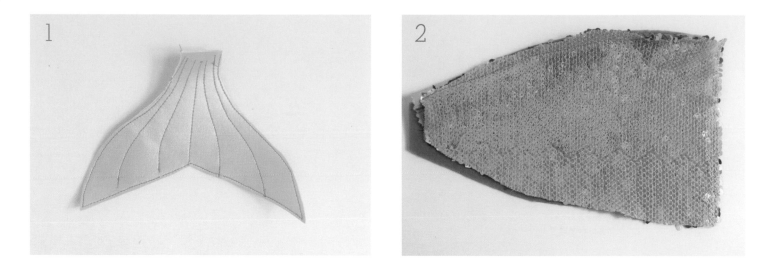

Step 1

Cut out the templates on page 63. Cut two fin pieces from the gold faux leather, two tails from the sequin fabric, and two tails from the blue cotton. Place the two fin pieces right sides together and tape them together to hold in place. Mark lines down the fin with pencil, then sew down the lines using contrasting thread.

Step 2

Now layer up the pencil case. Place one of the sequin pieces face up. Put the zipper on top, face down, with the top edges lined up. Place a lining piece on top, face down. Pin and sew together along the top of the zipper using the zipper foot on the machine.

Step 3

Place the second piece of sequin fabric on the table face up. Place the zipped piece on top with the unsewn edge of the zip lining up with the edge of the sequin fabric, as before. Pin the lining fabric on top, face down. Check the layers are in the correct order; they should be sequin, sequin, lining, lining. Sew as before, along the top of the zipper. When you open the piece out you should have the two sequin pieces with the zipper in the center.

Step 4

Open the zipper halfway. Take the sequin pieces so that they are right sides together and the inner pieces so they are also right sides together. Pin then sew all the way around the edge of the pencil case with a ½in (1cm) seam allowance, leaving the bottom of the tail open (where the fin goes) to allow you to turn the fabric.

Step 5

Turn the case the right way out through the gap, then insert the fin into the end, fold in the fabric, and hand sew the fin in place.

Step 6

To make the pull for the zipper, draw a starfish onto shrink plastic using the template on page 7. It should be about 6in (15cm) wide. Color it in using permanent pens or coloring pencils. The colors will darken as the plastic shrinks, so pick light colors.

Step 7

Cut out the starfish and punch a hole in one of the limbs. Shrink the shape in the oven as per the manufacturer's guidelines. The plastic will shrink and curl up. Don't remove it until it has laid back flat.

Step 8

Add a coat of varnish to the starfish and leave to dry. Attach a split ring to the hole in the plastic and attach the starfish to the zipper.

Starfish template

Copy at 200%

You could use standard sequined fabric if you prefer, although it's not as satisfying!

7

MERYL
THE MERMAID

This doll is made from felt and yarn and will make a very happy addition to any mermaid's bedroom. We used a sewing machine for this project, but you could sew by hand if you prefer — it will just take a little longer!

You will need

- Scissors
- 4 x sheets of purple felt, 8 x 12in (20 x 30cm)
- 2 x sheets of skin-colored felt, 8 x 12in (20 x 30cm)
- Scraps of green and pink felt for bikini and cheeks
- Pins
- Sewing machine
- Yarn for hair

- Pencil
- Blue and red embroidery thread for eyes and mouth
- Toy stuffing
- Needle and sewing thread
- 3 x small shell beads and 6 x pony beads for necklace
- Thin elastic for necklace
- Stick-on pearls or gems
- 2 x shell sequins
- Craft glue

Mermaids and mermen appear in folklore all over the world, including Europe, Asia, and Africa

Step 1

Cut out the templates on page 64 from felt. You will need two tails and two fins in purple and one green bikini. From skin-colored felt, cut two body pieces, then cut one front head and two back head pieces.

Step 2

Use the template on page 63 to cut rows of scales from purple felt. You will need about 25 pieces. Pin them onto the tail, starting from the bottom and working up. Overlap each piece so that no fabric underneath is visible.

Step 3

Starting at the bottom, sew the scales to the tail along the straight edge of each scale, removing pins as you go.

Step 4

For the hair, wrap yarn about 50 times around a book that is about 10in (25cm) wide. Pull the yarn off the book and cut through both ends of the loop to create two sets of strands.

Step 5

Take the first set of strands and pin along the long straight edge of one of the back head pieces, with the ends of yarn lined up with the fabric edge. Repeat for the other head piece. Sew just along the edge of the fabric to keep in place. Pin the two back head pieces together along the straight edge, with the yarn in between. Sew along the straight edge with a ½in (1cm) seam allowance. Trim the excess.

Step 6

Pin the back head piece and back body piece right sides together with the neck edges lined up and the hair tucked down out of the way. Sew together with a ½in (1cm) seam allowance. Join front head and front body piece in the same way.

Step 7

Wrap the yarn around the book 50 times again. Cut both ends of the loop as before, then pin the strands around the top of the front face piece, with the ends of the yarn lined up with the edge of the felt and the yarn covering the face. Sew just along the edge to hold in place.

Step 8

Sew the bikini onto the front body, using three lines of stitching on each side of the bikini to resemble a shell. Pin the front (scaled) tail and front body pieces right sides together with the top of the tail and bottom of the body lined up. Sew together with a ½in (1cm) seam allowance. Repeat for the back tail and body. Note that the pieces need to mirror each other.

Step 9

Pin the tail fin pieces together. Use a pencil to mark out decorative lines, as shown in the picture, on the front of the fin. Sew along these lines, then sew around the very edge of the tail to secure the front and back pieces together. Trim any excess fabric. (If you aren't using a sewing machine, use just one piece of fabric and backstitch the pattern on.)

Step 10

In pencil, mark the eyes and mouth on the face. By hand, backstitch the eyes using blue embroidery thread and the mouth in red. Cut ½in (1cm) circles out of pink felt for cheeks and hand stitch in place with pink thread.

Step 11

Place the two doll pieces right sides together with the hair pinned out of the way. Sew around the doll with a ½in (1cm) seam allowance, leaving 3in (8cm) on one side of the tail and the bottom of the tail open.

Step 12

Trim the fabric edges to ¼in (5mm), then snip into the felt all the way round to prevent puckering. Turn the doll out through the gap, then stuff.

Step 13

Slipstitch the opening on the side of the tail closed, tucking in loose ends. Tuck the fin into the bottom opening and pin. Backstitch in place by hand.

Step 14

Divide the hair so there is an even amount on each side and it covers the back of the head. Use pieces of yarn to tie the hair into bunches.

Step 15

Finally, thread beads onto a piece of elastic and tie it around the neck. Glue sequins and pearls onto the bikini and belly and add a shell bead to the doll's hair.

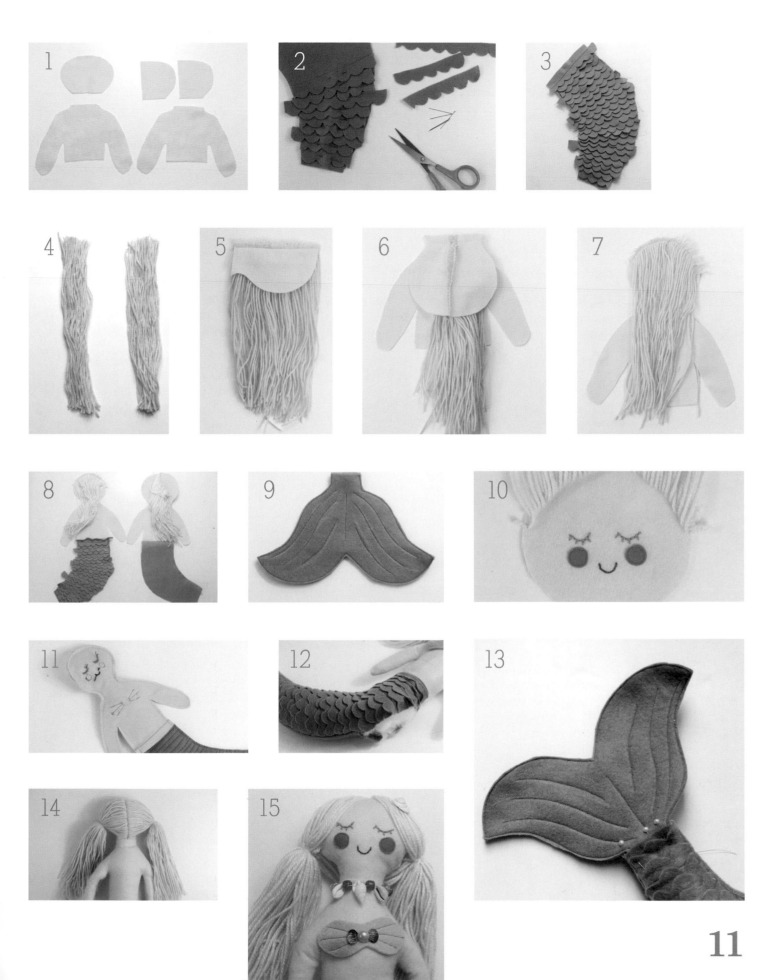

CLAMSHELL TRINKET BOX

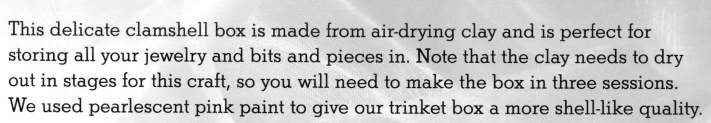

This delicate clamshell box is made from air-drying clay and is perfect for storing all your jewelry and bits and pieces in. Note that the clay needs to dry out in stages for this craft, so you will need to make the box in three sessions. We used pearlescent pink paint to give our trinket box a more shell-like quality.

You will need

✴ Rolling pin

✴ 17oz (500g) air-drying clay

✴ Plastic wrap

✴ Pencil

✴ Sharp knife

✴ 8in (20cm) piece of string

✴ 2 x dishes, about 6in (15cm) in diameter

✴ Fine-grit sandpaper

✴ Pearlescent pink and yellow acrylic paints, and paintbrush

✴ Scissors

✴ Scrap of yellow felt for hinge

✴ Craft glue

✴ Small round mirror, about 2in (5cm) in diameter (optional)

✴ 12 small shells to decorate mirror

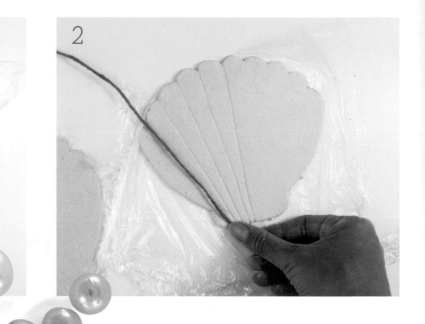

Step 1

Roll the clay out between two sheets of plastic wrap to ¼in (5mm) thick. Cut out the template on page 63 and place it on top of the plastic wrap over the clay. Draw around it with pencil to create an indentation. Remove the plastic wrap, then cut out the two clay shells with a sharp knife.

Step 2

Remove the top layer of plastic wrap and smooth the clay a little with your fingers dipped in water to remove any rough edges. Place the string onto the clay and press along it to create markings from the corners of the scalloped edge to the base of the shell.

Step 3

Put some plastic wrap into two small dishes. Then place one piece of clay, markings side down, into each dish. Push down gently with your fingers and leave to dry overnight.

Step 4

The clay should now be leather-hard but still a little malleable. Take the shells out of the dishes and place one on top of the other, with the backs and the edges lined up. Leave to dry out completely for another day.

Step 5

Using sandpaper, gently sand the shells down, inside and out. Be careful: if you press too hard, the clay will break.

Step 6

Using the acrylic paints, paint the outsides of the shells pearlescent pink and the insides yellow. Leave to dry.

Step 7

To make a hinge, cut a piece of yellow felt measuring 1½ x 2in (4 x 5cm). Glue one narrow end along the inside back of the shell and leave to dry. Then glue the other end in the corresponding place on the other shell.

Step 8

Glue the mirror inside the lid, then add small shells all the way around the mirror to frame it. Overlap the shells and the edge of the mirror slightly and leave for the glue to set.

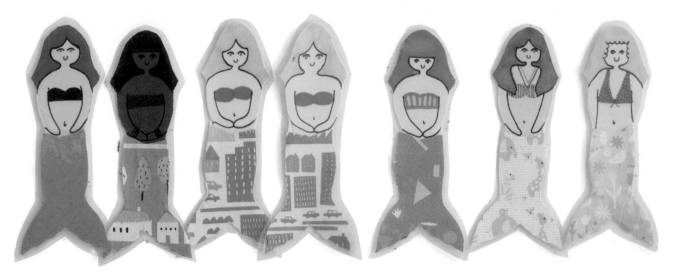

MERPAIRS GAME

Kids will love making and playing this mermaid pairs game, and they could even design their mermaids to look like friends and family. The box is decorated using bubble printing, which is a fantastic rainy-day activity for bored kids.

You will need

- Approximately 3 x sheets of skin-colored card, 8 x 12in (20 x 30cm)

- Scraps of paper in 12 different patterns

- Scissors

- Craft glue

- Coloring pens

- Sticky-backed plastic

- Cardboard box about 6in (15cm) wide

- White paint and paintbrush

- Bubble solution and wand (1 bottle should be enough)

- Paint palette

- 3 shades of food coloring

- Bowl of water

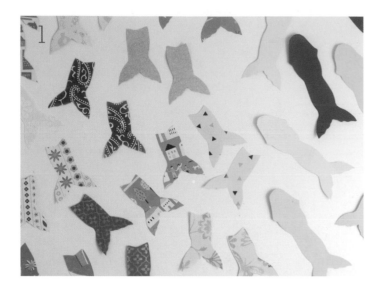

Step 1

Using the templates on page 63, cut out the mermaid bodies from skin-colored card. Then cut out the tails from the patterned paper. We made 12 matching pairs (24 mermaids). You can make more or fewer cards, as long as there is an even number and two of each design.

Step 2

Glue the tails onto the mermaid bodies, ensuring that you make pairs that match in skin color and tail design.

Step 3

Color the mermaids in with pens. Make sure that each mermaid in a pair is drawn and colored the same. Give your mermaids colorful hair, pretty bikinis, jewelry, and different expressions to make them really stand out.

Step 4

Cut out a piece of sticky-backed plastic large enough to fit all your mermaids on. Peel off the backing and place the mermaids on top. Spread them out so there is about a ½in (1cm) gap between each mermaid.

Step 5

Take another piece of sticky-backed plastic, the same size as before. Start at one end and carefully spread it over the mermaids, smoothing out any air bubbles. Cut each mermaid out, leaving ¼in (5mm) of plastic around the edges.

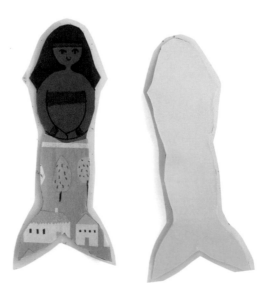

Step 6

Paint the cardboard box white and leave it to dry. To make the bubble effect on the box, pour a small amount of bubble solution into three or four different sections of a paint palette (use a number of small pots if you don't have a palette). Add the food coloring and mix.

Step 7

Head outside (or far away from soft furniture and carpets!) and put your box onto a piece of newspaper. Get a bowl of water and set it next to the box. Dip the wand into one of the colors and blow it onto the box to create a bubbly, splattery effect. Dip the wand in the water before using the next color to keep them separate. Make sure your box is completely covered in the bubble prints. Leave to dry.

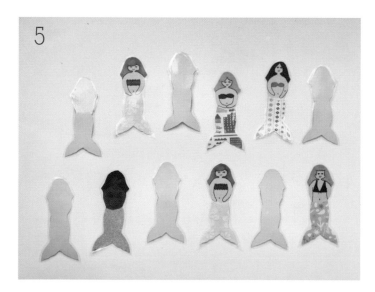

To play the game

Place all the mermaids face down on a table. Take it in turns to flip over two mermaids at a time to try to find a matching pair. Any pairs you find, you keep. Keep going until all the pairs are found. The winner is whoever has the most mermaids at the end.

MERMAID BLANKET

Get warm, snug, and ready listen to aquatic tales (or tails!) with this fleece mermaid tail blanket. The blanket should be long enough to reach to your child's chest: this blanket, made for a five-year-old, is 40in (1m) long. A sewing machine is required for this project.

You will need

- 80in (2m) of dark purple fleece
- 60in (1.5m) of pale purple fleece
- 40in (1m) of pink fleece

- Scissors
- Pins
- Tailor's chalk
- Sewing machine
- Coordinating sewing thread and lighter color sewing thread

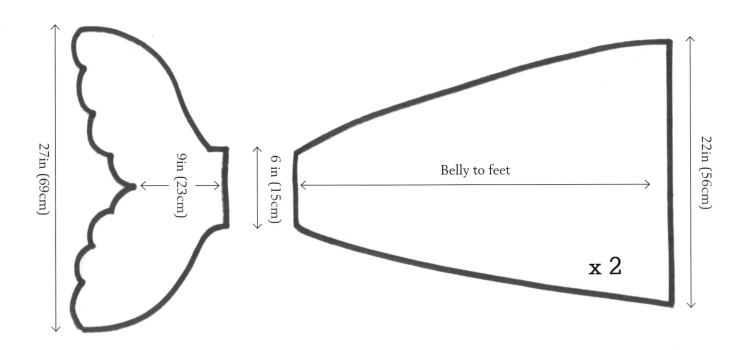

27in (69cm)

9in (23cm)

6 in (15cm)

Belly to feet

22in (56cm)

x 2

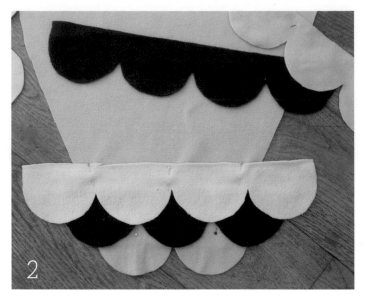

Step 1

Using the diagram on page 20 as a guide, draw out the main body of the blanket onto the piece of dark purple fleece, using tailor's chalk. Cut it out, then cut out another identical piece from pale purple fleece. Using the diagram as a guide, draw and cut out the fin from the dark purple fleece.

Step 2

Use the template on page 62 to cut rows of scales from each color of fleece. Vary the size of the rows to fit across the blanket at each point. Start at the bottom and pin the scales onto the front piece, overlapping the scales and alternating colors as you work your way up.

Step 3

Starting from the bottom, sew along the top straight edge of the scales, moving the overlapping scales out of the way as you go. Repeat to sew all the scales in place.

Step 4

Trim the excess scales off the sides of the blanket, following the line of the main piece underneath.

Step 5

Cut two strips of dark purple fleece measuring 4 x 30in (10 x 75cm). Fold and pin one strip over the top of the scaled blanket piece to conceal the raw edges. Sew ¼in (5mm) in from the edge of the strip. Repeat for the plain blanket piece.

Step 6

Pin the blanket pieces right sides together. Sew along both sides with a 1in (2.5cm) seam allowance. Trim the excess fabric. Keep the bottom of the blanket open.

Step 7

Use tailor's chalk to mark decorative lines onto the tail fin. Sew over the lines using a lighter color of thread.

Step 8

Sandwich the tail fin into the bottom of the blanket, with an overlap of 1in (2.5cm). Lift the bottom row of scales out of the way, then sew from the top of the blanket, with a ½in (1cm) seam allowance.

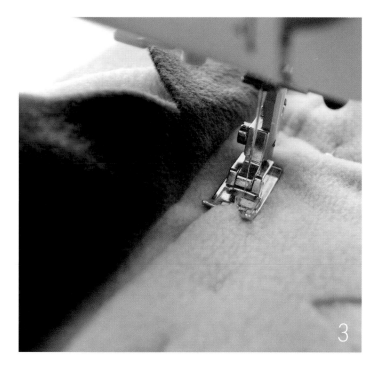

REEF WREATH

This wreath makes a great addition to any mermaid's bedroom door. You can buy clay starfish and shells online or in craft stores. If you live near a beach, you might be able to collect the shells yourself, which is much more fun!

You will need

- Dinner plate, about 12in (30cm) in diameter
- Piece of foam board, about 15in (40cm) square
- Green, white, and blue acrylic paints and paintbrush
- Sheets of red and white felt, 6 x 8in (15 x 20cm)
- Scissors
- Red yarn for large pompoms
- Handful of twigs
- Craft glue

- Strong glue
- Mixed selection of small and large shells, including 3 large ones
- Silver glitter
- Sheets of yellow and blue craft foam, 6 x 8in (15 x 20cm)
- Small clay starfish (optional)
- Selection of small ready-made pompoms
- Short piece of thin ribbon to hang the wreath

Step 1

To make your wreath base, use a large dinner plate to draw and cut a circle from foam board. Inside this, draw and cut out a smaller circle, about 7in (18cm) in diameter, to create a ring. Paint the ring green for the base color and leave to dry.

Step 2

Use the templates on page 62 to cut out a selection of about 20 coral shapes from red and white felt.

Step 3

To make the pompom sea urchins, wrap the red yarn around your hand approximately 50 times. Slip the yarn off your hand and tie another piece tightly around the middle. Cut through the looped ends and trim the pompom but leave them a little uneven to resemble urchins. Make 6.

Step 4

Paint some twigs white and leave them to dry, then arrange and glue them onto the wreath along with the felt coral and pompom sea urchins. Leave gaps to add the shells later.

Step 5

Cover the small shells with a coat of craft glue. Sprinkle them in silver glitter and leave to dry.

Step 6

Paint the large shells white and leave to dry. Paint the bottoms of the shell blue, then mix with a little white and blend up the shell by dabbing the paint on with a dry brush. Sprinkle a little glitter around the bottom and leave to dry.

Step 7

Use the templates on page 62 to cut out some mermaid tails from blue and yellow craft foam. Arrange these with the remaining items you have made on your wreath. When you are happy with the design, glue in place.

Step 8

Fold the piece of ribbon in half to form a hanging loop and glue to the back of the wreath.

SEASHORE GARDEN

This little beach is a mermaidy take on a fairy garden, and is really easy to make. You can pick up blue glass pebbles from online retailers for the sea, or you could just opt for the sandy beach. Make the mermaid doll first to allow her to dry out overnight while you make the garden.

You will need

- 9oz (250g) of air-drying clay
- 1 large pebble
- Cocktail stick
- Pen lid
- Rolling pin
- Selection of acrylic paints and paintbrushes
- Shallow pot, about 10in (25cm) in diameter
- About 2 cups of blue glass pebbles or beads
- About 5 cups of play sand
- 2 small succulent plants
- Popsicle/lolly stick
- Small twig
- Craft glue
- Small pebbles, shells, and starfish to finish

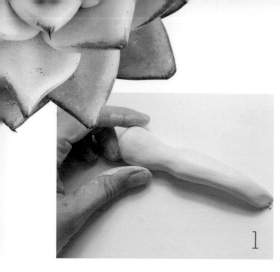

1

2

3

Step 1

Begin by making your mermaid doll. Roll a sausage of air-drying clay with a tapered end and a slightly pinched middle to resemble a body shape. See the accompanying image for an idea of the size.

Step 2

Bend the clay in the middle so that the doll can sit on the large pebble. Shape the top half so that it has a neck and shoulders and smooth the bottom half into a tail running along the pebble.

Step 3

Roll two smaller sausages for arms and press these onto the shoulders. Use your fingers to blend the joins.

Step 4

Roll a ball for the head. Shape to form a nose and use a cocktail stick to make a smiling mouth. Press the head onto the neck and blend the joins.

Step 5

Press two small balls of clay flat onto the mermaid for a bikini. Use a pen lid to press scales into the tail. Roll out a thin circle of clay, about 3in (8cm) in diameter and ⅛in (3mm) thick. Cut a slice out of it that is the width of the face (like a pizza) and position it onto the head for the hair. Press it down so that the clay forms natural folds. Trim any excess.

Step 6

Roll a piece of clay out to about 4in (10cm) and ¼in (6mm) thick. Cut the tail fin from the clay and score markings onto it with the cocktail stick. Press it under the bottom of the tail. Leave the mermaid on her rock to dry out overnight.

Step 7

Once the mermaid has dried, paint her any colors you like.

Step 8

For the garden, pour the glass pebbles into a third of the shallow dish, keeping them to one side with your hands. Pour the play sand into the rest of the pot. Dot some of the pebbles onto the sand.

Step 9

Take the succulents out of their pots and plant them in the sand. Cover the top of the soil with sand to hide it. Give them a little water.

Step 10

Make the beach sign by cutting a popsicle stick in half, then cutting off the rounded ends. Glue both pieces to the top of a twig and paint the sign to give the name for your beach.

Step 11

Place the mermaid in the garden on her pebble along with the sign, some smaller pebbles, starfish shapes, and small shells.

4

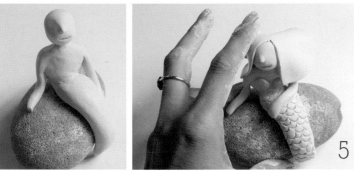

5

6

7

8

9

10

Make sure you keep your plants watered for a happy mermaid garden.

11

SHELL NECKLACE

No mermaid is fully dressed without a pretty shell necklace. This one is made from cardboard tubes, paper plates, and paper, so it's probably not a good idea to go swimming in the sea while you're wearing it!

You will need

- Scissors
- 2 x cardboard tubes
- 1 x paper plate
- Craft glue
- String
- 1 x sheet of white paper, 8 x 12in (20 x 30cm)
- Pencil and ruler

- Wooden skewer
- Parchment paper
- Pearlescent pink and green acrylic paints, yellow acrylic paint, and paintbrush
- Selection of stick-on pearls in different sizes
- Tweezers (optional)
- About 30in (80cm) length of fine elastic
- Small plastic beads

Step 1

Use the templates on page 63 to cut out the shell shapes. Cut two small and two medium shells from a cardboard tube. Cut the large shell from a paper plate, lining up the bottom of the shell with the ridged edge of the plate.

Step 2

Cover one of the shells with glue. Add a line of string down the center and bend it back round leaving a ¼in (6mm) loop for hanging at the base. Add string to the rest of the shell to resemble ridges, as shown in the picture. When the glue has dried, trim off any excess string.

Step 3

To make the paper beads, use a pencil and a ruler to draw triangles right across the length of the paper. The triangles should measure 1½in (4cm) at the widest end. Cut these triangles out. You will need about eight.

Step 4

To turn the triangles into beads, spread glue on one side of the paper, leaving 1in (2.5cm) unglued at the wider end. Place a skewer at this end and slowly roll up the paper around it. Remove the skewer and place the bead on parchment paper to dry.

Step 5

Paint the shells – pearlescent paint creates a pretty effect. To create an ombré effect, paint the top of the shell one color and the bottom another color. Mix the paint a little on a palette and dab it onto the shell so that the colors blend.

Step 6

Paint the paper beads to match the necklace and leave to dry.

Step 7

Add a few pearls to the bottom of each shell. If you have tweezers, use them to pick up the pearls, dip them in glue, and place them onto the shells. Leave the glue to dry.

Step 8

Thread the shells onto the elastic, along with the paper beads and the plastic beads, in whichever design you like. Here we have put the largest shell in the center with the smaller shells on the outside. Measure the necklace around your neck to work out the sizing, then tie the elastic and trim the excess.

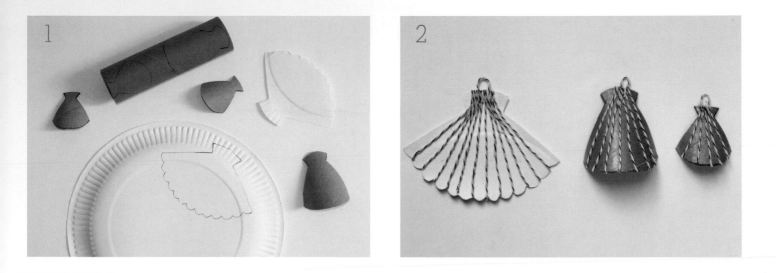

BUTTON ART T-SHIRT

This is a really easy craft that kids can happily get involved with. They will love to see the shape evolving from the buttons. You don't have to do a mermaid tail, you could do anything you like — a seahorse, shell, waves or any other shape as long as it is not too complicated.

You will need

Why not make some button art glued onto paper to frame as well? (See page 64 for mermaid template.)

- Tailor's chalk/pencil
- Plain cotton T-shirt
- 2 handfuls of pastel-colored buttons
- White sewing thread
- Hand-sewing needle
- Embroidery hoop (optional)
- Blue embroidery thread
- Letter-size/A4 piece of paper or card
- Tweezers
- Stick-on pearls
- Fabric glue

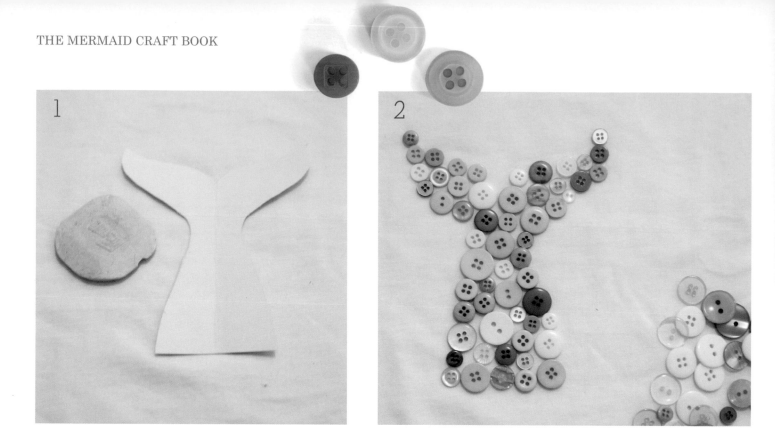

Step 1

Use the template on page 64 to draw a mermaid tail onto a piece of paper. Use tailor's chalk or a pencil to draw around the tail onto the middle of the T-shirt, with the fin at the top. If you're using pencil, draw a very light line.

Step 2

Remove the paper and arrange the buttons roughly within the tail outline on the T-shirt. If you like, you can take a picture to use in the next step for reference.

Step 3

Stitch the buttons in place by hand. If you have one, use an embroidery hoop to make the sewing easier.

Step 4

Remove the hoop if using. Don't worry if there are any gaps, as they will be filled in with pearls.

Step 5

Use tailor's chalk or pencil to draw a few wavy ocean lines at the bottom of the tail. Use blue embroidery thread to backstitch the lines in.

Step 6

Place a piece of card inside the T-shirt to protect the back. Fill any gaps in the tail with the pearls, fixing them with fabric glue. To make it easier, you can use tweezers to pick up the pearls, dip them in glue and place them onto the T-shirt.

Remember to only handwash the T-shirt in future to preserve the design.

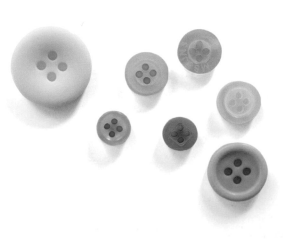

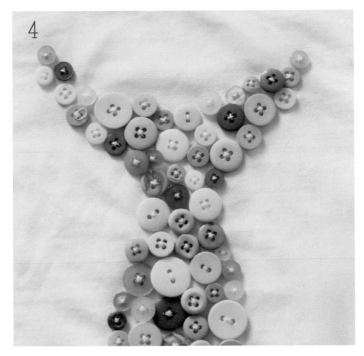

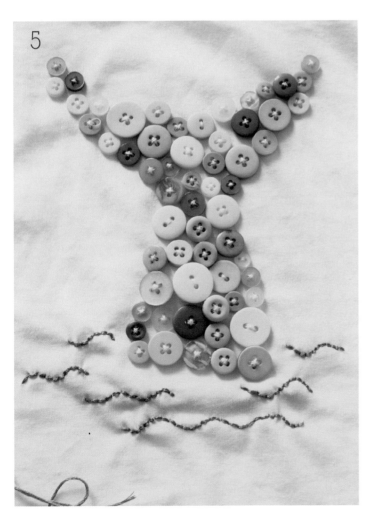

TRITON'S CROWN AND SPEAR

All rulers of the sea need a crown and spear to complete their royal aquatic duties. Kids will love getting their hands messy helping with the papier-mâché for these makes. Bear in mind that the crown and spear will need time to dry, so this project should be made over a few sessions.

You will need

- 2 x pieces of corrugated card, about 25 x 35in (65 x 90cm)
- Scissors
- Masking tape
- 3 x sheets of craft foam (any color), 6 x 8in (15 x 20cm)
- Craft glue
- 4 or 5 sheets of newspaper
- Gold paint and paintbrush
- Selection of shells in various sizes
- Selection of gems and pearls in various sizes and colors
- About 40in (1m) of string

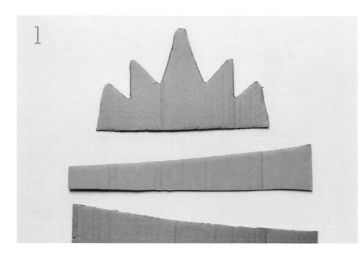

Step 1

Use the crown template on page 63 to cut out the front section of the crown from corrugated card. Cut two strips of card measuring roughly 2in (5cm) wide and 10in (30cm) long. The strips can taper slightly if you like, as shown in the picture.

Step 2

Attach the strips to each side of the crown with masking tape. Curve them round with your fingers. Test the crown on your child's head for size, then trim the strips so that there is only a slight overlap.

Step 3

Cover the inside and outside of the crown with craft foam. Glue the foam on and cut it to the shape of the crown. Check the sizing again, then fix the crown together with masking tape.

Step 4

For the spear, place the template from page 63 at the top of the corrugated card, leaving room for the handle. Draw around it and add a handle measuring about 2 x 18in (5 x 45cm). Cut it out and use to draw another spear on the other piece of card.

Step 5

Glue the spear pieces together. Cover the front, back, and sides in craft foam as with the crown.

Step 6

Make the papier-mâché paste by mixing two parts craft glue to one part water. Tear newspaper into small pieces and cover the crown and spear completely on all sides. Leave to dry overnight and apply a second coat of papier-mâché. When the papier-mâché is dry, paint it gold.

Step 7

Take a selection of shells and gems and stick them onto the front of the crown and spear in a design you like.

Step 8

Paint the string gold and leave it to dry. Arrange it around the bottom of the crown so that it hangs down like chains, as in the picture. Cut and glue in place.

Triton is a mythological Greek god of the sea. He would use a conch shell as a trumpet, which he would play to calm the waves or cause a storm, depending on his whim.

AQUARIUM PUPPETS

Create these cute mermaid families and their sea creature friends with their very own aquatic stage to perform on. An adult's shoebox with a removable lid is ideal for this project.

You will need

- Large shoebox with removable lid
- Craft paint in various colors and paintbrush
- Scissors
- 1 x piece of yellow card, 8 x 12in (20 x 30cm)
- Craft glue
- Craft foam in a range of colors, including skin colors and a mix of greens
- Black pen
- Cardboard egg carton

- Scraps of ribbon and trimmings, approx. 4in (10cm) long
- 4 small googly eyes
- Embroidery thread and needle
- 1 or 2 pieces of plain card, 8 x 12in (20 x 30cm)
- Scraps of different colored yarn for the mermaids' hair
- Coloring pens
- Wooden skewers

Step 1

Paint the shoebox inside and out. This one is an aquatic turquoise but you can go for any color you like. Once it is dry, draw a 1½in (4cm) border around the lid, cut the center out and discard. Repeat for one of the long sides of the box to create an opening to allow you to insert the puppets.

Step 2

Use the template on page 63 to cut out a scalloped trim from yellow card. The trim needs to be long enough to fit around the border in the lid. Fold over the straight edge onto the inside of the lid, leaving the scalloped edge on the outside, and glue in place.

Step 3

Use the templates on page 62 to cut out coral shapes from different shades of green foam. Glue onto the corners of the lid for decoration.

Step 4

Draw a little aquatic scene inside the shoebox to create a backdrop for the theater. This could be an aquarium, a mermaid palace, or just blue and bubbles – however simple or complex you like. Paint the scene and leave to dry. Go over the outlines in black pen to make it stand out.

Step 5

To make the jellyfish, cut out one of the bottom segments of an egg carton. Cut it in half and round the edges to make two jellyfish heads. Paint these pink and leave to dry. Then pierce a hole in the tops with scissors or a skewer. Glue scraps of ribbon to the base of each jellyfish and add googly eyes.

Step 6

Knot one end of a piece of embroidery thread. Pass the thread through the top of the jellyfish, then through the top of the theater so that the jellyfish hang down at the sides of the box. Glue the lid of the shoebox back in place at the front of the theater.

Step 7

To make the puppets, use the templates on page 62 to cut out the shapes from craft foam. You can cut as many characters as you like. Glue the tails onto the bottom of the bodies and add a bikini to the mommy mermaids.

Step 8

Glue all the mermaids and sea creatures onto pieces of card and cut them out.

Step 9

To make the mermaids' hair, wrap some yarn around three fingers about ten times. Cut through one end of the loop and glue it to the top of the heads. You can tie the hair into any style you like or trim it short once the glue has dried.

Step 10

Draw faces onto the mermaids and sea creatures. Glue a wooden skewer to the back of each puppet, halfway down, with the blunt end of the stick coming up at the top so that you can lower the puppets into the theater.

MERMAID TAIL

Transform into a merperson quicker than you can say "under the sea" with this fabric and duct-tape tail. Ideally, you can make this project using a sewing machine, but you could always glue the scales on if you don't have one.

You will need

- ⭐ 40in (1m) length of shiny fabric
- ⭐ Duct tape in 4 or 5 pastel or sparkly colors
- ⭐ Scissors
- ⭐ 20 x sheets of white card, 8 x 12in (20 x 30cm)
- ⭐ Pins
- ⭐ Sewing machine
- ⭐ 3in (8cm) piece of sew-on Velcro (hook and loop tape)

In olden times, people mistook certain human-sized sea creatures, such as manatees and dugongs, for mermaids. This strengthened the belief that mermaids existed

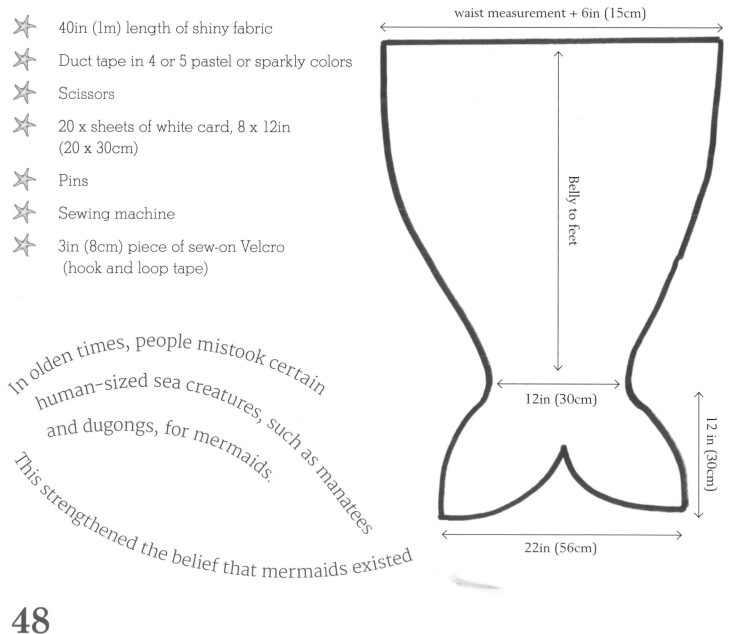

waist measurement + 6in (15cm)

Belly to feet

12in (30cm)

12 in (30cm)

22in (56cm)

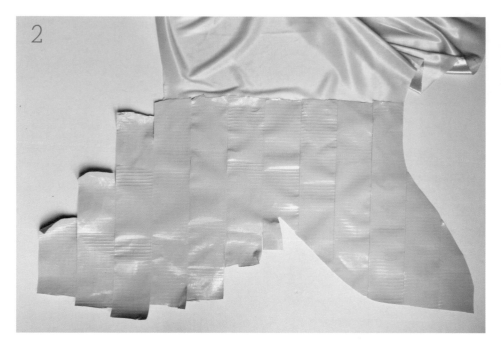

Step 1

Use the diagram on page 48 as a guide to draw a mermaid tail onto the shiny fabric. Measure your child from their belly to their feet for the measurement for the tail. For the waist measurement, measure around the waist and add on 6in (15cm) so the tail overlaps when it is worn.

Step 2

On the reverse of the fabric, cover the tail fin part in vertical strips of duct tape. Neaten up the edges with scissors.

Step 3

To make the scales, cover sheets of card with duct tape. Use the template on page 63 to draw scales onto the reverse of the card. Cut them out. You'll need approximately 200 scales.

Step 4

Pin a row of scales along the top of the duct tape fin with the corners of the scales touching. Sew in place along the straight edge of the scales using a sewing machine.

Step 5

Continue in the same way to fill the tail up with scales. When you are nearing the top of the fabric, stop 3in (8cm) from the top.

Step 6

Trim the scales along the sides of the tail for a neat edge.

Step 7

Fill up the remaining fabric at the top of the tail with sparkly duct tape, covering the top of the scales a little to hide the edges. Fold the tape over to the back of the fabric to conceal the raw edge of the fabric.

Step 8

Measure the tail on your child. The tail should wrap around the back and meet with an overlap at the front. Mark where you need to put the Velcro (hook and loop tape) on the overlap. Pin in place, then sew along the edges of the Velcro.

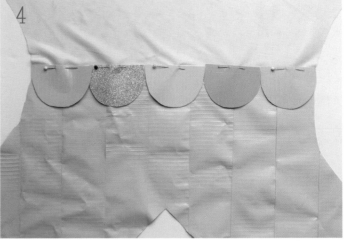

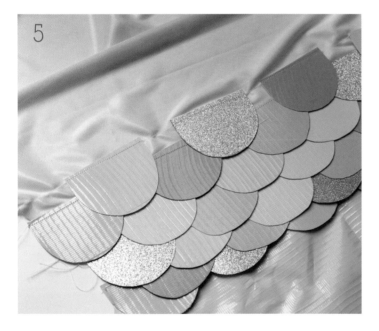

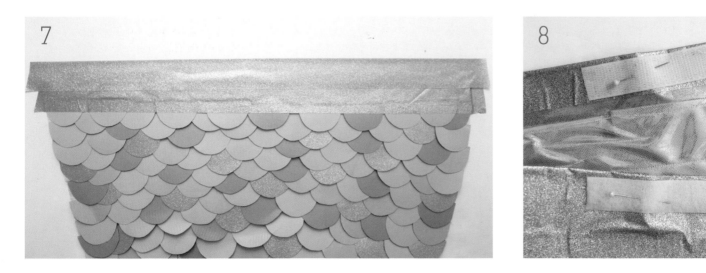

OCEAN SLIME AND MERDOUGH

This under-the-sea slime is mesmerizing and shimmers like mermaid scales. Store it in an airtight container and it will last for a few weeks. Please note that the recipe requires borax substitute, which can cause irritation. Make sure you wash your hands after making or playing with your slime and, of course, do not eat it! For little merpeople, there's also a super speedy recipe for aquatic playdough.

You will need

For the ocean slime:

- ½ cup clear PVA glue
- Water
- 1 tsp borax substitute powder
- About 3 tsp glitter (preferably biodegradable) in mermaidy colors (e.g. silver, blue, turquoise)

For the merdough:

- Mixing bowl
- 2 cups plain flour
- ½ cup salt
- 1½ tbsp cream of tartar
- 1 cup boiling water
- 1 tbsp oil
- Gel food coloring in turquoise, pink, and purple
- Cocktail stick or teaspoon
- Shells, sequins, and sea-themed cookie cutters

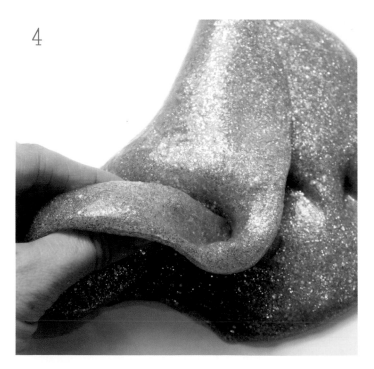

Ocean slime

Step 1

Pour the glue into a mixing bowl. Add ½ cup of water and mix until thoroughly combined.

Step 2

Add the glitter and stir it in.

Step 3

Add 1 teaspoon of borax substitute to 1 cup of water and stir thoroughly. Gradually add the borax solution to the glue mixture, 1 teaspoon at a time, stirring continuously. You will see that the mixture starts to get gloopy. Keep adding the borax solution until the slime just comes away from sides of the bowl – this should happen with about 8-10 teaspoons of solution.

Step 4

Now you can get your fingers into the slime and start mixing. If the mixture is still sticky add a little more solution. If it goes too hard, knead in some warm water until it is the consistency you want.

Merdough

Step 1

Mix together the dry ingredients in a large bowl. In a separate bowl mix together the water and oil.

Step 2

Pour the liquid into the dry ingredients and beat until combined. Knead into a dough using your hands. If the dough feels sticky add a little flour and if it is cracking add a few drops of water.

Step 3

Separate the dough into three roughly equal pieces. Use a cocktail stick or the end of a teaspoon to drop a little food coloring onto each piece.

Step 4

Fold the coloring into the dough, kneading until combined. Add more coloring for a more intense color.

Step 5

Turn your merdough into an ocean scene using shells, sequins and sea-themed cookie cutters.

MERMAID CAKE

This little fondant mermaid is almost too good to eat — although she's made from pure sugar, so you may not want to bite into her anyway! The wavy sea, sandy beach, and chocolate sea creatures are easy to create, making this cake the perfect centerpiece for any under-the-sea party.

You will need

- 2 x 8in (20cm) cake pans
- Parchment paper
- 12oz (350g) softened butter
- 12oz (350g) superfine/caster sugar
- 6 medium eggs, beaten
- 1 tsp vanilla extract
- 12oz (350g) self-rising flour
- 3 tsp baking powder
- 28oz (800g) vanilla buttercream
- 9oz (250g) white ready-to-use fondant
- Plastic wrap
- 3 small plain cupcakes

- 1oz (25g) green ready-to-use fondant
- 1oz (25g) red ready-to-use fondant
- Black, red, brown, blue, and yellow gel food coloring
- Fine paintbrush
- Cocktail stick or toothpick
- Cake board
- 2oz (50g) light brown sugar
- 2oz (50g) ground almonds
- Chocolate writing icing
- Decorative sprinkles (optional)

Step 1

To make the cake, preheat the oven to 350°F (180°C). Grease and line the cake pans. Mix the butter and sugar until light and creamy, then slowly add the eggs, mixing each one in. Add the vanilla extract, then sift the flour and baking powder into the mixture and fold in. Divide between the cake pans and bake for 35-40 minutes. Remove from the oven and allow to cool on a wire rack.

Step 2

Measure 10oz (300g) of buttercream. Spread some on top of one of the cakes and sandwich the two together. Add the rest all over. At this point you can freeze the cake, defrosting the day before the party.

Step 3

For the rock, mix 3oz (100g) white fondant with a little black food coloring and blend to create a marbled gray, then roll out between two sheets of plastic wrap. Pull the paper off the cupcakes and stack them in the center of the fondant. Loosely wrap it around the cakes and place on a piece of parchment paper.

Step 4

To make the mermaid, mix a 2in (5cm) lump of white fondant with a small amount of red or brown food coloring, to get a skin color. Roll a marble-sized piece out for a head, then roll some arms and a torso. Roll a tail and cut a fin shape from green fondant. See the image to understand the size and shapes.

Step 5

Attach the torso to the tail, using a tiny dab of water to glue together. Bend the fondant in the middle to give a sitting appearance. Push the cocktail stick into the rock, sharp side up, where you want to locate the mermaid. Then push the body onto the cocktail stick so that it runs up the center of the torso and out the top. Add the head, arms and fin to the mermaid, again using a little water.

Step 6

Roll out some red fondant for the hair and cut a circle out of it. Then cut a quarter of the circle out.

Step 7

Place it on the head. Press it down and snip into the fondant to allow it to fall easily. Trim to give her a neat haircut.

Step 8

Use a fine paintbrush and food coloring to paint a face on the mermaid and give her a shell bikini.

Step 9

To make shells, mix a little red into white fondant to make pink. Roll into a sausage with one thin and one fat end. Twist it around a cocktail stick, then use the end of a teaspoon to push an indent into the big end.

Step 10

For a starfish, roll 5 small pieces of red fondant and join together, then use the tip of the cocktail stick to push dots into the icing. Pop the mermaid, shells and starfish into the fridge until you are ready to put them on the cake.

Step 11

Mix 10oz (300g) of buttercream with blue food coloring until you get a good sea shade. Don't mix it in too well as it's good to have a marbled effect. Put the cake onto a cake board. Spread the buttercream onto the top of the cake in a crescent shape, roughly, for a wave effect. Add buttercream around the sides underneath the blue. Reserve a little of the buttercream for later.

Step 12

Spread the remaining plain buttercream on the rest of the cake. Mix the light brown sugar with the ground almonds. Sprinkle and press onto the plain buttercream on the cake to resemble sand.

Step 13

Use the remaining blue buttercream to make waves going onto the sand.

Step 14

Use chocolate writing icing to draw fish shapes onto a piece of baking parchment. Once the chocolate has set, peel them gently off and attach to the sides of the cake.

Step 15

Position the mermaid on her rock onto the cake and add the shells. You can then add some decorative sprinkles for a finishing touch.

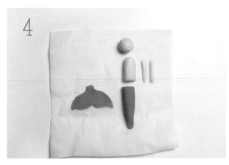

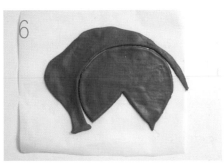

UNDER-THE-SEA PARTY

An under-the-sea party is easy to put on with the help of our handy guide. Below are some useful ideas for mermaid-themed party food, games, and décor. For the perfect centerpiece, turn to page 56 to make a mermaid cake.

Food

There are loads of sea-themed food available, from chocolate seashells to fish-shaped nuggets. Cookie cutters are a quick way to add an underwater twist. Cut sandwiches into stars to look like starfish, or use a seahorse cutter to make cookies and decorate them with pearly icing sugar.

Mermaid wands

These can be made by adding fruit to a wooden skewer and topping with a watermelon star.

Seashell pasta

To create seaweed, add some green food coloring to a pan of salted boiling water, then cook spaghetti or tagliatelle. Cook shell-shaped pasta in a separate pan and stir in cooked peas and sweet corn. Combine both pastas with a little olive oil and serve.

Croissant crabs

These can be made by filling mini croissants with cheese or ham, then adding a couple of cocktail sticks with googly eyes glued to the ends. Cut carrots into pincer shapes and add them to the sides of the croissants using more cocktail sticks. Arrange the crabs on a bed of lettuce seaweed.

Oyster shells

These are made by adding a swirl of pink buttercream to the bottom of a round cookie, then popping a round candy in the center. Add another cookie to the top and press one side down to resemble an open shell.

Games & activities

Make a mermaid

Cut out a selection of mermaid bodies, tails, and hair from colored card. Lay out on the table with glue sticks and bowls of googly eyes, sequins, gems, and pens and let kids assemble their own merpeople.

Hunt the pearl

Paint foam balls with pearlescent paint. Hide them around the garden or house and ask children to see who can find the most pearls.

Pin the fin

Draw, paint, and cut out a large finless mermaid onto a piece of card. Cut out a separate fin from card, add adhesive putty to the back, then let children take it in turns to pin their fin onto the mermaid while they are blindfolded.

Decoration & extras

Party hats

Give party hats an aquatic theme. Draw round a dinner plate on a piece of card, cut the circles out and cut in half. Draw scales on, then twist the card to form a cone. Cut cardboard fins and glue to the top, then add a little elastic to keep the hat in place.

Jellyfish

Paint a selection of paper bowls, then glue googly eyes onto the outside rims and add crêpe paper strips, ribbon, or trimmings to the bottoms. Add a loop to the center to hang up.

Bunting

Cut layers of pearly card into starfish, seashells, or mermaid tails. Punch holes into the sides and thread onto string to create beautiful bunting.

Buckets and spades

Serve food in toy buckets with spades instead of serving spoons for a beachy vibe. You could also fill buckets with party favors instead of using bags.

Party favors

Add starfish name labels to party bags or buckets and fill with bubble wands, fortune fish, shell jewelry, and tubs of Ocean Slime (see page 52).

TEMPLATES

Templates shown at actual size can be traced and cut out, or photocopied. For templates that have been reduced in size, enlarge them on a photocopier to the percentage stated. Position each template as near to the top left-hand corner of the photocopier glass as possible. You may need a few goes to find the best position.

Reef Wreath and Aquarium Puppets
(see pages 24 and 44)
Copy at 150%

Mermaid Blanket
(see page 20) Copy at 200%

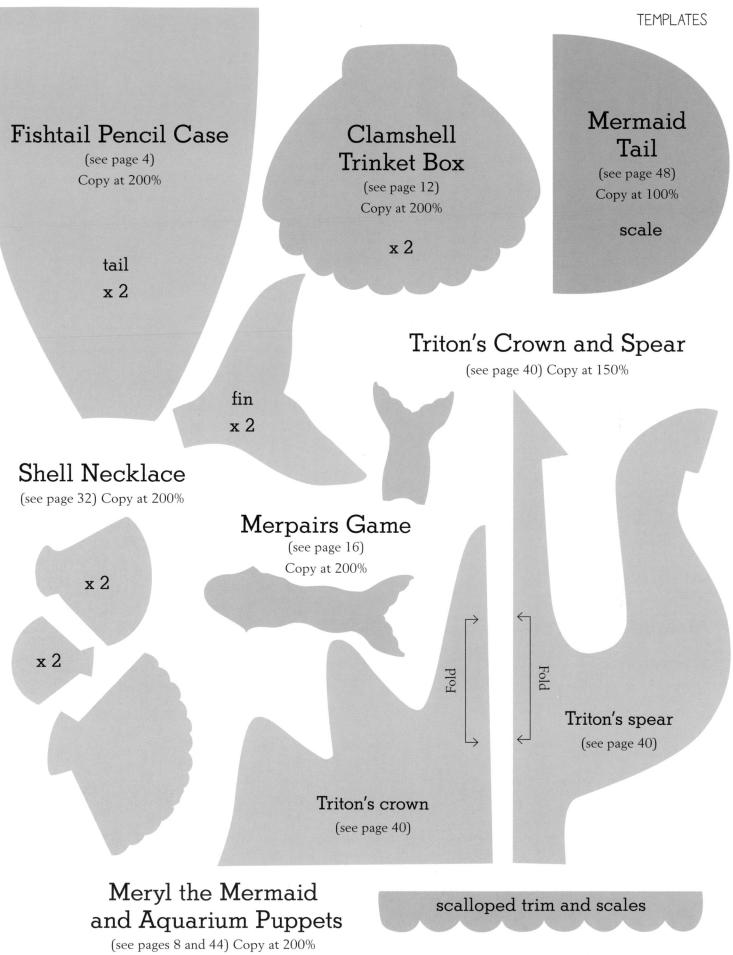

Fishtail Pencil Case
(see page 4)
Copy at 200%

tail
x 2

Clamshell
Trinket Box
(see page 12)
Copy at 200%

x 2

Mermaid
Tail
(see page 48)
Copy at 100%

scale

fin
x 2

Triton's Crown and Spear
(see page 40) Copy at 150%

Shell Necklace
(see page 32) Copy at 200%

Merpairs Game
(see page 16)
Copy at 200%

x 2

x 2

Fold

Fold

Triton's spear
(see page 40)

Triton's crown
(see page 40)

Meryl the Mermaid
and Aquarium Puppets
(see pages 8 and 44) Copy at 200%

scalloped trim and scales

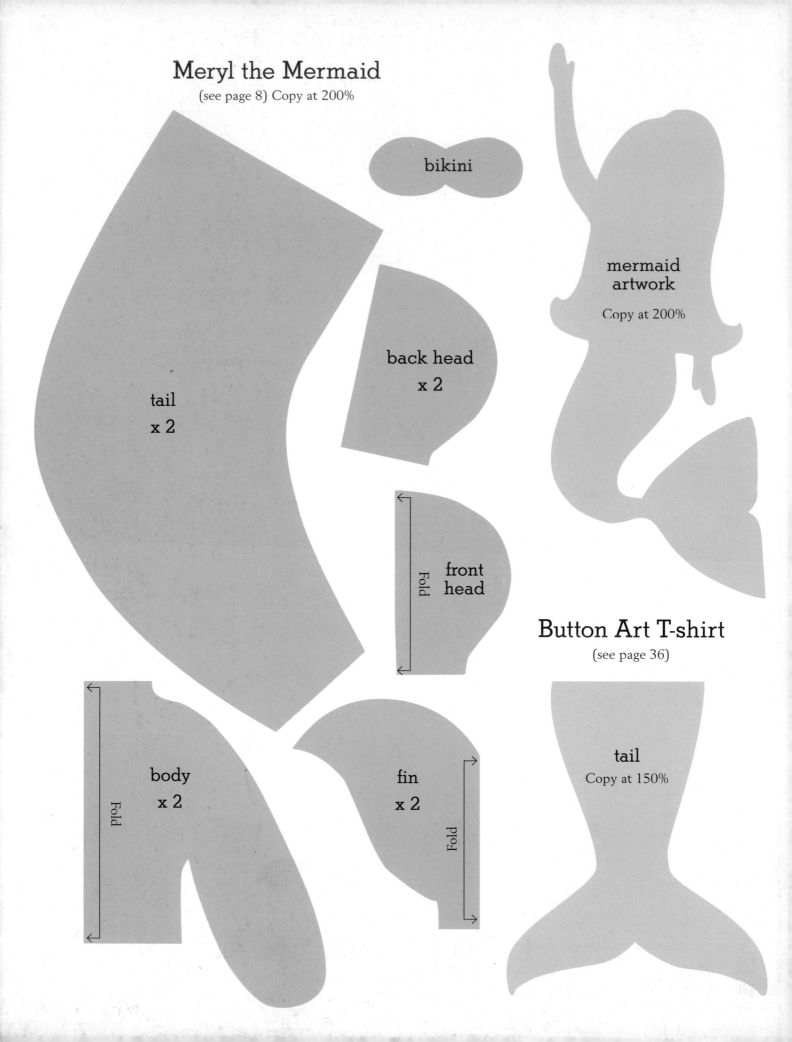

Meryl the Mermaid

(see page 8) Copy at 200%

bikini

mermaid artwork

Copy at 200%

tail
x 2

back head
x 2

front head

Fold

Button Art T-shirt

(see page 36)

body
x 2

Fold

fin
x 2

Fold

tail
Copy at 150%